Living Unapologetically

How I Learned to Break Social Norms, Set Boundaries, and Finally Put Myself First by embracing selfcare

Rowan Blake

Contents

The Year I Stopped Saying Yes v

Part One
The First No's—Breaking the Habit of Yes

1. My First Real No 3
2. No to Obligatory Socializing 6
3. No to Toxic Relationships 9

Part Two
The Liberation of No

4. Saying No at Work (Without Getting Fired) 15
5. No to the Hustle, Yes to Rest 19
6. No to Social Niceties 23

Part Three
The Cost of No

7. The Fallout—Losing People, Losing Comfort 29
8. No to Mindless Distractions 32

Part Four
The Ultimate Test of No

9. The Final Challenge 37
10. The Aftermath—Life Beyond the Experiment 39

The Next Adventure 42

The Year I Stopped Saying Yes

It started with a calendar.

Not a fancy, leather-bound planner, not a sleek productivity app—just the basic one on my phone. One evening, after another long day of doing things I didn't want to do, for people I wasn't sure I even liked, I opened it up and stared at the endless sea of dots. Every little circle, every highlighted event, every reminder was something I had agreed to.

Dinner with an old coworker I hadn't seen in years? Check. Helping my neighbor's cousin's dog-sit for the weekend? Yep. Attending a networking event I had no actual desire to be at but convinced myself was "good for my career"? Oh, absolutely. I scrolled and scrolled, and the dots kept coming. I had built an entire life around saying **Yes**—to invitations, obligations, extra work, unnecessary favors, even group chats I never wanted to be in.

And then it hit me: **I didn't actually want to do half of these things.**

I wasn't busy—I was just really bad at saying **No**.

The Breaking Point

The real tipping point came at a baby shower. Not mine, obviously.

I was there for a woman I barely knew—**a plus-one to someone else's obligation.** I found myself sitting at a pastel-draped table, nodding enthusiastically while a group of women debated the relative merits of organic cotton onesies. At some point, as a diaper-themed game was being explained in far too much detail, I had an out-of-body experience.

What the hell am I doing here?
I had been so conditioned to agree to things—out of politeness, guilt, or some warped sense of social responsibility—that I had ended up at a baby shower for a near-stranger, eating cake I didn't want, pretending to care about swaddle fabric.

On the drive home, still clutching my unwanted party favor (a mini jar of bath salts, because apparently, we were celebrating someone else's baby by encouraging our own self-care), I decided I was done.

For **one full year**, I would say **No**. No to things I didn't want to do, no to obligations that drained me, no to people who took more than they gave, no to the guilt that came every time I tried to set a boundary.

The Rules of No
I knew if I was going to do this, I needed rules—because if left to my own instincts, I'd probably find myself back at another baby shower in three weeks.

Here's what counted as a **hard No**:

- Unnecessary social events. If I didn't genuinely **want** to go, I wasn't going.
- Unpaid emotional labor. No more being the friend-therapist, the unpaid event planner, the problem solver for other people's messes.
- Work projects beyond my job description. No to extra tasks disguised as "great opportunities."
- Mindless commitments. No to every favor that made my stomach clench before I even finished saying "Sure, no problem."

Of course, I couldn't say **No** to everything. Bills still had to be paid. My mother's calls still had to be answered (selectively). But the goal was simple: **If it didn't bring me joy, fulfillment, or a direct paycheck, I was out.**

One Year, One Word

I expected some resistance. I knew people would be surprised—maybe even a little annoyed. I had spent **a lifetime** being agreeable, easy-going, the "sure, I'll do it" person. What would happen when I started saying **No**?

Or, just maybe, would I finally **breathe**?

This is the story of what happened when I stopped saying **Yes**—and started reclaiming my time, my energy, and my sanity. A year of boundaries, awkward conversations, lost invitations, and (spoiler alert) the best sleep I've had in my adult life.

Welcome to **Living Unapologetically**
 A Year of Saying No.

Part One
The First No's—Breaking the Habit of Yes

My First Real No

My First Real No

It was a Tuesday afternoon when I encountered my first real test. Not a dramatic, life-changing moment—just a simple, seemingly harmless request.

"Hey, could you help me out with something real quick?"

It was my coworker, Sarah, standing in my doorway, laptop in hand, looking frazzled. She was always **frazzled**, running around the office like a woman whose to-do list was actively chasing her. Normally, I would have sighed internally, plastered on a helpful smile, and said **Yes**, despite the fact that "real quick" in Sarah's world translated to **at least an hour** of unpaid problem-solving.

But not today.

This was **Day One** of my **Year of No.**

So, I took a deep breath, steadied myself, and—without thinking too hard—said it.

"I can't, sorry."

And then... silence.

Sarah blinked at me, confused. I blinked back, equally confused. I had no follow-up, no excuse, no justifiable reason other than **I simply didn't want to.**

She waited, probably expecting me to cave, to fill in the awkwardness with a "but maybe later?" or "if you really need me..." But I held firm. My face was neutral, my body language calm. On the outside, I looked like a person who knew how to set boundaries.

Inside? **Pure panic.**

Had I just ruined our work dynamic? Would she think I was rude? Selfish? A terrible human being? My heart pounded as she shifted her weight, her lips pursed in clear disappointment.

"Okay," she said finally, turning away. "I'll figure it out."

And then, just like that, **she left.**

She **figured it out.**

A shocking revelation: **the world did not end.**

The Aftermath: Guilt, Doubt, and a New Discovery

For the next hour, I felt **awful**. I imagined Sarah at her desk, grumbling about me. I imagined my boss overhearing the interaction and making a mental note: *Wow, she's not a team player.*

But then—about two hours later—I walked past Sarah's desk. She was **fine**. Laughing at a joke, typing away, fully unbothered. She had, indeed, **figured it out.**

And I had **an entire extra hour** where I wasn't stuck fixing someone else's problem.

For the first time, I felt something I didn't expect. Not just relief, but a tiny, rebellious **thrill**.

I had said **No.**

And **nothing bad happened.**

Well, except for the fact that now I had to rethink my entire life.

Why Had This Been So Hard?

Why did something as small as declining a favor make me feel like I had committed a crime? **Why was saying "No" so difficult for me?**

The answer: **Years of conditioning.**

I had spent my entire life being **nice**. The good friend, the good coworker, the easygoing person who didn't make waves. **Saying "No" felt unnatural because I had spent years believing that my value came from being available.**

Nice girls don't say No.

Hard workers don't say No.

Good people don't say No.

But maybe—**just maybe**—they should.

The First No Changes Everything

That single, seemingly insignificant "No" unlocked something in me. It made me realize just how much of my time I had been giving away **without even questioning it.**

Would Sarah have helped me if the roles were reversed? Maybe. Maybe not. But that wasn't the point. The point was **I had a choice.** And I had never actually exercised it before.

And so, the next time an invitation landed in my inbox, one that I would have previously accepted out of habit, I hesitated. **Did I actually want to go?**

Spoiler alert: **I did not.**

And this time, saying **No** felt just a little bit easier.

Little did I know, I was just getting started.

No to Obligatory Socializing

The first real test of my commitment to **saying No** came in the form of an **evite**—which was honestly rude, because I hadn't even mentally prepared myself for the next challenge yet.

"Hey! We're all getting together this weekend! You HAVE to come!"

No, I really didn't.

It was a group dinner for someone's birthday—someone I liked but wasn't particularly **close to.** The kind of invite where your presence wasn't really required, but declining still felt weirdly personal. In my past life as a **chronic Yes-er**, I would have RSVP'd **yes**, mentally prepared myself for an evening of polite conversation, overpriced cocktails, and pretending to be fascinated by someone's recent home renovation.

But this time? **No.**

The Anxiety of Saying No

I hovered over my keyboard for an **embarrassingly long time** before typing out my response.

"Hey, thanks for the invite! I'm going to sit this one out, but have a great time!"

And then, just to be **extra sure** my rejection didn't make me sound like a horrible person, I added:

"Let's catch up soon!"

You know, to **soften the blow** of my completely reasonable decision to not attend a social event I had no real interest in.

I hit send. And immediately felt **like a monster.**

Would they think I was rude? Unfriendly? Would they talk about me at dinner, whispering about how I had *changed*? (This, by the way, is a truly ridiculous fear because people are mostly concerned with their own lives, not obsessing over who skipped dinner.)

My phone buzzed. A response. I braced myself.

"No worries! Hope to see you soon!"

...That was it?

No guilt trip? No dramatic, "We never see you anymore!"? No passive-aggressive, "Well, I guess we'll miss you" with a crying emoji?

Apparently, **I had built up the consequences of saying No way more than reality ever would.**

The Discomfort of Missing Out

Of course, just because I said No didn't mean the evening was **entirely stress-free.** Around 7:00 PM, the guilt started creeping in.

I pictured everyone laughing, clinking glasses, snapping group photos. Was I missing out? Would I regret this? Would they form new inside jokes that I wouldn't be part of?

I did what any rational adult would do—I **stalked their Instagram stories.**

The verdict? The usual: a dimly lit restaurant, a couple of cocktails, a group selfie with the caption **"Love this crew!"**

And I? **Was in my pajamas. Eating takeout. Watching TV.**
And I felt... relieved.

Because the truth is, I **didn't** want to be there. The only reason I had ever wanted to go was to avoid the guilt of saying No.

Why Was I Saying Yes to Things I Didn't Even Want to Do?

I realized that **I had spent years accepting invitations out of obligation, not genuine desire.**

- I said **Yes** because I didn't want people to think I was rude.
- I said **Yes** because I was afraid of being left out.

- I said **Yes** because I thought that's what "good friends" did.

But the truth? **A good friend shows up because they actually want to be there—not because they feel guilty.**

The Freedom of No

That night, as I curled up on my couch with a blanket and zero regrets, I realized something:

Saying No to things I didn't want to do **meant saying Yes to myself.**

Yes to rest.

Yes to energy.

Yes to the people and activities that actually mattered.

And the best part? No one cared as much as I thought they would.

This was my first big step toward **radical boundaries.**

Next up? **Saying No to the relationships that were draining me dry.**

That one... was going to be much harder.

- The coworker who trauma-dumped over coffee breaks but never asked how I was.
- The person who always wanted to "catch up" but left me emotionally drained every time.

I started **saying No** to them. And every time, it got a little bit easier.

Here's what I learned:

1 Good friends respect boundaries. The ones who don't? Probably weren't great friends to begin with.

2 People show you who they are when you stop meeting their expectations. If someone disappears because you stopped overextending yourself? **They were never really there for you either.**

3 Cutting out the wrong people makes space for the right ones. Once I stopped spending energy on draining friendships, I had more time for the relationships that actually made me happy.

Emotional Detox: Making Room for Better Connections

By the time I had cut out a few toxic connections, I started noticing something incredible:

I felt **less resentful** and **more at peace.**

Instead of spending hours listening to someone else's problems, I used that time to **read, rest, and actually take care of myself.**

Instead of forcing myself to text people who wouldn't have done the same for me, I **nurtured the friendships that truly mattered.**

And, most importantly, I realized that **saying No wasn't selfish. It was self-respect.**

Next up? **Saying No at work—without losing my job.**

This one was going to take some strategy.

Part Two
The Liberation of No

Saying No at Work (Without Getting Fired)

If there was one place I had perfected the art of **reluctant Yes-ing**, it was the workplace.

Need someone to stay late and finish a project? **Sure!**

Could you just handle this "one extra thing"? **Of course!**

Would I be open to taking on a new responsibility for the same salary? **Absolutely! Sounds like a great opportunity!**

I had spent **years** saying Yes to everything because that's what "good employees" do, right? They're **team players.** They're **helpful.** They're **reliable.**

They're also **exhausted.**

By the time my **Year of No** rolled around, my to-do list looked like a **corporate sacrifice ritual**—except the only thing getting sacrificed was **me.**

And I had finally decided to stop volunteering for it.

The First Workplace No

The first opportunity to test my newfound backbone came in the form of an **email from my boss.**

"Hey! Can you put together a quick report on X for the team by Friday?"

I read it twice. This was **not** in my job description. This was **not** something I had time for. This was **a classic case of 'quick' actually meaning 'at least five hours of extra work.'**

Old me? Would have responded instantly with **"Of course! Happy to help!"** while silently weeping.

New me? **Paused.**

Then, I typed:

"Hi [Boss's Name], I'd love to help, but I'm currently at capacity with my existing workload. If this is a priority, could we discuss what should be deprioritized to make room for it?"

And then I hit send.

And then I stared at my screen, fully convinced that I had just signed my own termination papers.

The Unexpected Response

Fifteen minutes later, my boss replied:

"No worries! I'll assign it to someone else."

...Excuse me?

That was it? No **passive-aggressive follow-up?** No **reminder that we're all busy?** No **impromptu meeting about 'teamwork' and 'going the extra mile'?**

I had just freed up five hours of my life with one email.

Was this the corporate equivalent of discovering fire?

The Fear of Workplace No's

Before this experiment, I had been convinced that **saying No at work would get me labeled as difficult, lazy, or ungrateful.** But it turned out my boss **wasn't** some vengeful overlord waiting for me to slip up—**he just needed the work done and didn't care who did it.**

And yet, for years, I had **volunteered** myself for extra tasks that no one forced me to take.

Why?

Because I wanted to be seen as valuable.

Because I wanted to be liked.

Because I thought overworking was the same thing as being a good employee.

Newsflash: It's not.

The Art of the Professional No

Once I realized **I wasn't actually required to say Yes all the time,** I started experimenting with different versions of No at work.

• **The Prioritization No:** "I'm at capacity right now. Which of my current tasks should I put on hold to take this on?"

• **The Delegation No:** "I think [Coworker's Name] might be a better fit for this since they've worked on similar projects before."

• **The Boundary-Setting No:** "I don't check emails after 6 PM, but I'll get back to you first thing in the morning."

And you know what? **No one fired me.**

In fact, something unexpected happened: **People started respecting my time more.**

When you're the person who always says Yes, people assume you'll always be available. But when you **set boundaries,** they start **valuing your time.**

The No That Changed Everything

A few months into my experiment, my boss called me into a meeting.

"**We'd love for you to take on a new initiative,**" he said, smiling. "It's going to be a big project, but I think you'd be great for it."

I **almost** said Yes out of instinct. My brain **screamed**:

• *This is good for your career!*
• *What if he's testing you?*
• *You can figure out how to fit it in!*

But instead, I asked, **"Will there be a title change or a salary adjustment?"**

Silence.

"Well... no," he admitted. "But it would be great experience."

Ah. There it was. **The 'great experience' trap.**

I smiled politely and responded, **"I appreciate the opportunity, but at this point, I need to focus on my current workload."**

And just like that, I walked out of that meeting with **zero new responsibilities, zero extra hours of work, and zero regrets.**

Work Didn't Own Me Anymore

Saying No at work didn't mean I was slacking off—it meant I was no longer **giving away my time for free.**

I still did my job. I still worked hard. But I was no longer volunteering for **every single extra task** just to prove my worth.

Because my worth? **Didn't come from how much of myself I sacrificed.**

Next up? **Saying No to the Hustle Culture that told me I had to "earn" my rest.**

That one was going to be **personal.**

No to the Hustle, Yes to Rest

At some point in my life, I had absorbed a dangerous belief:
Rest is something you earn.
Not something you just... do.

No, no, no. Rest had to be **justified**—preferably with an itemized list of completed tasks, proving that I had suffered enough to warrant a break.

If I wasn't **exhausted**, I wasn't working hard enough. If I wasn't **busy**, I was falling behind. If I wasn't **hustling**, someone else was out there doing more, achieving more, getting further ahead while I sat around like a sloth with questionable life choices.

So, naturally, I had spent years glorifying **overwork**.

- **Being exhausted?** A badge of honor.
- **Working on weekends?** Just proving my dedication.
- **Burnout?** A completely normal part of success!

It wasn't until my **Year of No** that I realized just how **messed up** that mindset was.

The Productivity Guilt Struggle

The first time I actively chose **to do nothing**, I felt **physically ill.**

It was a Sunday afternoon. My to-do list was long, but none of it was urgent. I had this wild, rebellious idea:

What if... I just... rested?
Not a **fake rest** where I still secretly checked emails.
Not a **productive rest** where I read a self-improvement book.
Just... actual, guilt-free nothingness.
So, I put on sweatpants, made tea, and sat on my couch.
Within five minutes, my brain went into full **meltdown mode.**
• *Should I be meal prepping?*
• *Maybe I should do some reading?*
• *What if I just quickly check my inbox—just for a second?*
I physically **twitched** with the urge to be **useful.**

It took an **entire hour** before my nervous system finally accepted that **nothing was happening, and that was okay.**

By the end of the afternoon, something **magical happened**: I felt **calm.** Not stressed. Not frantic. Just **a person who had given themselves permission to exist without performing productivity.**

It felt **illegal.**

The No That Changed My Time

The next major shift came when I stopped **glorifying "being busy."**

For years, my default response to **"How are you?"** was:
"Oh, you know, just really busy!"
Because **busy** meant **important.**
Busy meant **productive.**
Busy meant **I was doing something with my life.**

But once I started **saying No** to unnecessary obligations, something strange happened—**I had more free time.**

And instead of **enjoying** that free time, I panicked.
• Was I not working hard enough?
• Was I failing?
• Was I falling behind?

I realized I had spent so many years **measuring my worth by my output** that I had no idea how to just **be.**

So, I made a decision:
I was going to start treating rest like a non-negotiable, not a luxury.

Setting Boundaries with Work & Time

I started with **one terrifying experiment**:

I **stopped answering emails after 6 PM.**

Let me tell you—**the first time I ignored an evening email, my hands shook.**

Would my boss be annoyed?

Would my coworkers think I was slacking?

Would the entire company collapse because I wasn't available 24/7?

The next morning, I checked my inbox... **and nothing had exploded.**

In fact, **no one had even noticed.**

So, I did something even more radical:

I **stopped checking work messages on weekends.**

And guess what? **Still no explosions.**

For the first time in **years**, my free time was actually **free.**

The Myth of More

Hustle culture teaches us that **more** is always better.

More hours.

More projects.

More side gigs.

But **what if more isn't better?**

What if **better is better?**

I had been so focused on **doing more** that I had never stopped to ask:

Do I actually enjoy my life?

Because here's the truth no one wants to admit:

Most of us aren't exhausted because we have too much work.

We're exhausted because we **never stop working.**

Saying Yes to Rest, Saying No to the Hustle Lie

By the time I fully embraced **rest without guilt**, something **shocking happened**:

- I was **more productive** at work (turns out, sleep is useful).
- I was **happier** in my personal life (because I actually had time for it).
- I was **less resentful** of my job, my commitments, and my existence in general.

Because I finally understood something hustle culture never teaches you:

You don't **earn** rest.

You don't have to **deserve** it.

You just **need it.**

Next up? **Saying No to the social niceties that were draining my energy.**

Because it was time to stop pretending I cared about small talk.

No to Social Niceties

I never realized how much of my social energy was spent on **obligation** rather than **genuine connection**.

For years, I had conditioned myself to be the person who always **nodded, smiled, and engaged**, even when I had no real interest in the conversation. I was the one who **filled awkward silences**, made people feel comfortable, and pretended to care about things that, in truth, meant nothing to me.

It wasn't that I disliked people. **I valued connection.** But I started noticing that most of my conversations were **performative** rather than meaningful. I wasn't speaking because I had something to say—I was speaking because I felt like I had to.

So I decided to stop.

What Happened When I Stopped Faking Enthusiasm

The first time I tested this, I was at work.

A colleague started telling me about a reality show they had been watching. Normally, I would have nodded, thrown in an **"Oh wow, really?"** at the right moments, and pretended to be engaged until the conversation ran its course.

But this time, instead of performing interest, I simply **listened**

without responding much. No forced questions, no polite interjections. If I had nothing real to say, I said nothing.

It was uncomfortable at first. The conversation **fizzled out quickly.** My colleague looked at me expectantly, waiting for me to carry it forward. When I didn't, the silence grew, and then—just like that—the conversation ended.

And I realized: **not every conversation needs to be stretched beyond its natural lifespan.**

I had been so used to keeping things going that I never considered what would happen if I didn't.

The answer? **Nothing bad.**

Walking Away from a Conversation I Didn't Want to Be In

The real test came at a social gathering.

I found myself cornered by someone who was enthusiastically explaining something I had no interest in. The old me would have **stood there, smiling, nodding, waiting for an opportunity to escape gracefully.**

But instead of pretending, I did something different.

I simply said, **"It was nice talking to you,"** gave a polite nod, and walked away.

At first, I felt a twinge of guilt—had I been rude? But then I reminded myself: **I wasn't obligated to stand in a conversation that drained me.** The person barely noticed my exit and immediately turned to someone else.

That was when it hit me—**most people aren't paying as much attention as we think they are.** The world doesn't stop when we excuse ourselves.

The Brutal Honesty Experiment: Only Speaking When I Meant It

One of the biggest shifts happened when I decided to **only speak when I truly meant it.**

- If I didn't care about a topic, I wouldn't fake enthusiasm.
- If I didn't have an opinion, I wouldn't force myself to contribute.
- If I wasn't interested in a conversation, I wouldn't pretend otherwise.

This didn't mean I became cold or detached—it meant I became **intentional.**

And an unexpected thing happened: **The quality of my conversations improved.**

Instead of empty small talk, I started having **real conversations.** Instead of stretching interactions beyond their natural length, I let them end when they were supposed to.

I had always thought **silence was something to be avoided.** But I learned that sometimes, silence is just space waiting to be filled with something real.

What I Learned from Saying No to Social Niceties

1 Not every conversation needs to be prolonged. If something naturally ends, it's okay to let it.

2 People don't notice your absence as much as you think they do. Walking away from a conversation won't cause a scene.

3 Speaking less makes the words you do say more meaningful. When you stop talking out of obligation, your words carry more weight.

Next up? **Saying No to distractions—the endless noise of social media, mindless scrolling, and wasted time.** Because if I was cutting unnecessary conversations in real life, it was time to do the same online.

Part Three
The Cost of No

The Fallout—Losing People, Losing Comfort

The Fallout—Losing People, Losing Comfort

Saying **No** wasn't just about setting boundaries. It was about breaking patterns.

And breaking patterns—especially ones that other people have come to expect—comes with consequences.

At first, I thought people would celebrate my new approach. I imagined friends admiring my strength, family respecting my independence, and colleagues seeing me as someone who was confident and self-assured.

What I didn't expect was **pushback.**

Not from strangers. Not from casual acquaintances.

But from the **people closest to me.**

The First Friend Who Got Angry

It started with a simple request.

A friend—let's call her **Emily**—asked me to help her move.

Now, if this had been a **true emergency**, I would have helped in a heartbeat. But this wasn't. She had movers, she had other friends, and she had given me exactly **one day's notice.**

Before my **Year of No**, I would have dropped everything, shown up early, and spent the whole day hauling furniture while telling myself, *This is what good friends do.*

But this time? I told her the truth:

"Hey, I can't help this weekend. I hope it all goes smoothly, though!"

That was it. No elaborate excuse. No over-apologizing. Just a simple **No.**

Her response?

"Wow. Okay. I guess I just thought you'd be there for me."

I stared at my phone, guilt creeping in. Old me would have immediately followed up with, *Wait, I'll try to make it work!* But I didn't.

Because here's what I realized: **If one 'No' ruins a friendship, then it was never a real friendship to begin with.**

We didn't speak for a while after that. And yeah, it stung. But it also showed me something important: **Some people only like you when you're saying Yes.**

The Family Argument That Nearly Ended in Silence

Friends were one thing. **Family was another.**

In my family, **boundaries were not a thing.** You answered every call, attended every event, and if you dared to decline? Well, you better have a **really good reason.**

So when I said **No** to a family dinner—just because I didn't feel like going—it caused **actual chaos.**

- **"Are you mad at someone?"** (*No.*)
- **"Is something wrong?"** (*Also no.*)
- **"You can't just skip family things for no reason."**

Apparently, **my personal time was not considered a valid reason.**

And when I calmly repeated, **"I just need some space today,"** my mother's response was, **"...I don't understand you anymore."**

That one hit differently.

Because **that's what happens when you change.** People who are used to a version of you—the always-available, always-agreeable version —**struggle when you become someone different.**

It took weeks before things felt normal again. But I didn't regret it.

Because I was done **performing obligation at the expense of my own peace.**

The Loneliness of Choosing Yourself

Here's what no one tells you about setting boundaries: **It can be incredibly lonely at first.**

When you start saying No:
- **Some invitations stop coming.**
- **Some people stop reaching out.**
- **Some relationships fade.**

And that's terrifying. Because for a while, **it feels like you made the wrong choice.**

There were moments where I sat in my quiet apartment, wondering if I had gone too far. If I had **pushed people away.** If I had made myself **too unavailable.**

But then, something amazing happened.

The people who truly cared? **They stayed.**

They adjusted. They accepted my boundaries. They didn't guilt-trip me.

And the ones who drifted? Maybe they were never really there for **me**—just the version of me that was convenient for them.

What I Learned from Losing People and Losing Comfort

1 Not everyone will like the new you—and that's okay. People who only stick around when you're overextending yourself? They were never your people.

2 You will feel lonely before you feel free. The space that boundaries create feels empty at first—but it makes room for something better.

3 Real connections survive No's. The right people don't leave just because you start protecting your time. They respect it.

Next up? **Saying No to distractions—the endless scrolling, the mindless spending, the noise I had used to escape.** Because if I was choosing myself, I needed to be fully present for it.

No to Mindless Distractions

No to Mindless Distractions
If I had mastered saying No to other people, the next challenge was saying No to **myself.**

Because for years, I had been filling every empty moment with **something.**

Scrolling. Clicking. Watching. Buying.

The constant flood of **noise, entertainment, and consumption** had become my default. And the more I cut back on unnecessary commitments and draining relationships, the more I realized...

I was still distracting myself.

So I decided to do something drastic: **cut out mindless distractions—starting with social media.**

The Day I Deleted Social Media for a Month

It wasn't a spontaneous decision. I had thought about it for weeks, hesitating every time.

Because, honestly? **I was afraid.**
- Afraid of missing out.
- Afraid of feeling disconnected.
- Afraid of sitting in silence with my own thoughts.

But I knew that if I truly wanted to break free from **auto-pilot habits**, I had to do it.

So one night, without overthinking it, **I deleted every social media app from my phone.**

And then? **Panic.**

Within the first few hours, I reached for my phone **at least 30 times**, my fingers automatically searching for Instagram. I caught myself unlocking my screen with no purpose, staring at it blankly before realizing **I had nothing to check.**

It was uncomfortable. Like losing a security blanket I hadn't even realized I was clinging to.

But after a few days, something shifted.

The urge to check my phone started to fade. My thoughts stopped feeling **so fragmented.** I started reading books again—not just for five minutes before bed, but for hours, uninterrupted.

I paid attention to things I hadn't noticed in a long time.

And the biggest realization?

I wasn't missing anything.

The endless updates, the curated posts, the constant stream of content—it had all **felt important** when I was in it. But stepping away made me see it for what it was: **just noise.**

Cutting Out Meaningless Spending, Empty Entertainment, and Impulse Choices

Social media was just the beginning.

Once I realized how much of my time was being **hijacked by distractions**, I started paying attention to my other habits.

• **Online shopping.** Clicking "Add to Cart" whenever I was bored, convincing myself that the next purchase would somehow make me happier.

• **Streaming endless shows.** Not because I truly enjoyed them, but because it was easier than sitting in silence.

• **Saying Yes to things I didn't even want.** An invite to an event? A sale that made me buy things I didn't need? I had been running on autopilot for years.

So, I started cutting back.

I deleted shopping apps. I stopped watching shows just to fill

time. I paused before every impulse decision and asked, 'Do I actually want this?'

And what I found was that most of the time, **I didn't.**

Most of the things I had been doing weren't bringing me joy or fulfillment. They were just **distractions from discomfort.**

The Battle with Boredom: What Happens When You Have No Distractions Left?

Here's the part I didn't expect: **without distractions, I had to actually sit with myself.**

And at first? **It was brutal.**

Boredom felt **foreign**—something I had spent years avoiding. My brain itched for something to do, some way to fill the space.

But over time, I started to appreciate it.

Because boredom wasn't emptiness. It was **possibility.**

It was in those quiet, undistracted moments that I started:

• **Writing again.** Not for work, not for anyone else—just for myself.

• **Reflecting on what I actually wanted.** Without the internet telling me what I should want.

• **Feeling present in my own life.** Instead of constantly trying to escape it.

What I Learned from Saying No to Distractions

1 Most distractions aren't relaxing—they're numbing. Scrolling, binge-watching, impulse shopping—they don't refresh us. They just keep us occupied.

2 When you remove distractions, you make space for what actually matters. Creativity, real rest, meaningful connection—it all happens in the quiet moments.

3 Boredom isn't the enemy. Sometimes, it's where the best things begin.

Next up? **Saying No to hustle culture—the idea that rest has to be 'earned' and that doing nothing is a waste of time.** Because if I had finally reclaimed my time, it was time to stop feeling guilty for how I used it.

Part Four
The Ultimate Test of No

The Final Challenge

By the time I reached the final stretch of my **Year of No**, I felt different. Lighter. More in control of my life. I had set boundaries, walked away from toxic relationships, reclaimed my time, and cut out distractions.

But I knew there was still one test left.

One final challenge that would prove whether I had truly changed—or if I would slip back into old habits.

The Ultimate Test

It came in the form of **an opportunity.**

A work opportunity, to be specific. One of those *"You'd be crazy to pass this up"* offers that people dream about. It was a promotion. More money. More visibility. More responsibility.

Old me would have said **Yes** immediately. Would have ignored the stress, the extra workload, the gut feeling that whispered, *This is not what you actually want.*

New me? Paused.

I sat with it. I weighed what I had learned.

And then, I did the one thing I never thought I'd do.

I said No.

Not because I was afraid. Not because I wasn't capable. But because **it didn't align with the life I wanted anymore.**

Reflecting on the Transformation

Saying No to that opportunity was **the hardest No of the entire year.** Not because it was difficult in the moment, but because it made me realize just how much I had changed.

If I had been given the same offer a year ago, I would have jumped at it—without thinking. I would have seen it as **progress**, as **validation**, as **proof of my worth.**

But now? I knew that success wasn't just about saying Yes to more. Sometimes, **real success is knowing what to walk away from.**

I had spent an entire year **learning how to protect my time, energy, and peace.** This was the moment I proved—to myself more than anyone else—that I meant it.

And the moment I turned down that offer, I felt something unexpected.

Relief.

No guilt. No second-guessing. Just **a deep knowing that I had made the right choice.**

What This Journey Was Really About

When I started this experiment, I thought it was just about learning to say No. But by the end, I realized:

- It was about **trusting myself.**
- It was about **choosing my own definition of happiness.**
- It was about **realizing that I don't owe my time to anyone— not my job, not my social circle, not even my past self.**

The real lesson wasn't just about boundaries—it was about **learning to live on my own terms.**

I had spent so much of my life trying to be **the reliable one, the agreeable one, the person who showed up even when they didn't want to.**

And by the end of this year, I was finally, **completely, unapologetically myself.**

Next up? **What happens when the experiment is over.**

Because after a year of radical change, I had to ask myself:

What comes next?

The Aftermath—Life Beyond the Experiment

The day my **Year of No** officially ended, I expected to feel something monumental.

Maybe a sense of victory. Maybe an overwhelming urge to celebrate. Maybe even the temptation to revert back to my old ways, to go on a saying-Yes binge just to make up for lost time.

Instead, I woke up, made coffee, and went about my day **like nothing had changed.**

Because the truth was, **everything had already changed.**

There was no finish line. No dramatic ending. Just the quiet realization that **this wasn't an experiment anymore—it was my life now.**

How Life Was Forever Changed

At the start of this journey, I had been trapped in a cycle of **obligation, burnout, and people-pleasing.** I had said Yes out of guilt, fear, or habit—never stopping to ask if I actually wanted to.

Now? Every decision, every commitment, every use of my time was **intentional.**

Some of the biggest shifts:

- **My calendar looked different.** Instead of being packed with plans I didn't want, it was filled with things I genuinely enjoyed—and empty space that I fiercely protected.

- **My relationships were healthier.** The people who remained in my life respected my boundaries. The ones who only valued me when I was overextending myself had naturally faded away.
- **I was less tired—physically, mentally, emotionally.** Saying No didn't just free up my schedule; it freed up my **energy**.

And perhaps the biggest change?

I no longer felt guilty for choosing myself.

The Hardest Lessons I Learned

1 Not everyone will understand your No—but that's not your problem.

Some people will be disappointed. Some will take it personally. But the right people? They'll respect it.

2 The fear of saying No is always worse than the actual No.

The overthinking, the guilt, the imagined worst-case scenario—it's almost never as bad as we think.

3 You don't need permission to protect your time.

You don't need to justify it. You don't need an excuse. "I don't want to" is a full sentence.

4 If a relationship, job, or commitment can't survive a No, it was never stable to begin with.

The right connections, opportunities, and friendships **won't crumble** just because you set a boundary.

Advice for Anyone Who Wants to Try Their Own 'No' Experiment

If I could go back and give myself advice at the start of this journey, here's what I'd say:

- **Start small.** You don't have to overhaul your life overnight. Practice with one No at a time.
- **Don't over-explain.** The more you justify, the more people push back. Keep it simple.
- **Expect resistance.** Not everyone will like the new version of you—and that's okay.
- **Pay attention to how you feel.** The best part of saying No isn't the time you gain—it's the peace you feel.

Saying No isn't about pushing people away or avoiding responsibility. **It's about choosing your life instead of letting it be chosen for you.**

Next? **What happens after the experiment ends—and why the next chapter of my life is one I'm writing completely on my own terms.**

The Next Adventure

The experiment is over.

One year of **saying No**—to obligations I didn't want, to people who drained me, to distractions that numbed me, to the idea that my time belonged to everyone but me.

So, what happens now?

The truth is, **I don't have a plan.**

And for the first time in my life, **that doesn't scare me.**

I used to believe that saying No meant missing out. That setting boundaries meant shutting people out. That if I stopped saying Yes, I would somehow be **less—less liked, less successful, less worthy.**

But now? I see it differently.

Saying No wasn't about **limiting my life.** It was about making room for the things that actually mattered.

What's Next?

I don't know what comes next—and that's the beauty of it.

Because instead of filling my time with things I feel obligated to do, I'm **leaving space for the things I actually want.**

• If I say Yes to something, it will be **because I truly mean it.**

• If I commit to something, it will be **because it aligns with the life I want to build.**

- And if I walk away from something, it will be **because I trust myself enough to know when it's time to let go.**

I've spent too many years being afraid of disappointing others. Now, my biggest fear is **disappointing myself.**

How This Experience Reshaped My Outlook on Life

I used to think that happiness came from **adding more—more plans, more commitments, more achievements.**

But after a year of radical boundaries, I realized:

- **Happiness isn't about how much you do—it's about how much of it actually matters.**
- **Rest isn't something you earn—it's something you need.**
- **The people who truly love you will respect your boundaries, not punish you for them.**
- **You are allowed to choose yourself—without apology, without guilt, without explanation.**

And perhaps the most important lesson?

Life isn't something you have to keep saying Yes to. It's something you get to shape. Something you get to say No to, when necessary.

Your Own 'No' Experiment

If you're reading this and feeling like you need a change, consider this your invitation.

Your own **Year of No** doesn't have to look like mine. Maybe it's a month. Maybe it's a week. Maybe it starts with just **one single No.**

But here's what I can promise you:

The first No will feel uncomfortable.

The second will feel rebellious.

The third will feel powerful.

And by the time you realize you've stopped apologizing for it? **You'll wonder why you ever waited so long.**

So, what happens next?

That's up to you.

And this time, **you get to decide.**

www.ingramcontent.com/pod-product-compliance
Lightning Source LLC
LaVergne TN
LVHW050027080526
838202LV00069B/6948